ETIQUETTE FOR
PROFESSIONAL ACTORS

Prudence Pickle Presents

ETIQUETTE
FOR
PROFESSIONAL
ACTORS

As told to Peggy O'Connell

Palmetto Publishing Group
Charleston, SC

Prudence Pickle Presents Etiquette for Professional Actors
Copyright © 2018 by Peggy O'Connell

First Edition

Printed in the United States

ISBN-13: 978-1-64111-170-6
ISBN-10: 1-64111-170-4

Contents

Foreword

It was the first day of rehearsal. Everybody was there, Luigi Oliveri "Bless-You" Bertrand, the great "Pauser" Piacenti and others—gods and goddesses of the theatre all.

They were doing *Hamlet* in Connecticut and the cast was all a-twitter about the young man playing the title role. Word had it that our leading man was fresh out of one of the top actor training programs in America, and he was nothing less than a GENIUS!

Wesley had just called roll and it was evident that the gifted young Hamlet was ten minutes late for the first rehearsal. The cast bantered about back and forth for a bit, the way brilliant and witty actors often do, and after a spell our star made his pathetic entrance. Apparently, his class at The Dolly Dinkle School of Dance had just run overtime. The big galoot then commenced to WHISTLE for what seemed like a fortnight.

My powder was beginning to moisten when the eeejut's whistling mercifully subsided, only to be succeeded by coughs and sneezes leveled at the entire acting company. Horrifying. Then his CELL PHONE rang like Cathedral bells.

His insolence continued as he cornered the distinguished old gentleman playing the ghost of Hamlet's father. (Did I mention I'm a ghost? More on that later!) But in a BIG, LOUD, DISCOURTEOUS VOICE right there inside the theatre, he asked the wizened old tragedian, "How much money did you make when you played MACBETH last year?" As soon as he said, "Macbeth," everybody ran for cover.

The lout then popped his gum and proceeded to inform the former ingénue, the lovely Bless You Bertrand, how he disagreed with the critic who called her a "TALENTLESS COW," sending poor Bless-You into a fit of the jerks.

As if all of this wasn't enough to drive one to drink, His Nibs then marched over to the lighting designer and asked him why his "last show was so ridiculously dark?"

So it was at this very moment, Dear Readers, that I, Prudence Pickle, decided to pen *ETIQUETTE for PROFESSIONAL ACTORS*. Although I am certainly not considered old, I do possess an oyster bed of knowledge from which we shall draw pearls. It is my pleasure, and my duty to pass along this priceless information to you.

After all, your defunct graciousness may very well be what's keeping you in the unemployment line.

Dear me, you wouldn't want to end up like that poor Hamlet fellow (whose career was soon shivered asunder), now would you?

Follow my Pickle rules of etiquette and allow your newly refined deportment to be the golden thread that connects you to the grand career you are meant to have.

CHAPTER ONE
Lesson Etiquette

1. When attending voice lessons, or any sort of private coaching, it would be lovely if you have your check written out prior to your arrival. This way, your teacher won't have to wait for it or request it from you.

2. If you're early for your lesson, wait in your vehicle, or if you're in a studio—down the hall. Lessons can be very personal, and students are expecting them to be private.

3. When attending a speech, voice, or acting lesson, it is imperative that you bring your own water bottle and recording device.

4. Understand that if you can't give your coach a twenty-four hours cancellation notice, you are required to pay for this lesson.

5. Instructors do not care to squander their time and talents, so practice, practice, practice. Teaching you will be akin to opening Christmas gifts!

6. Remove your hat when attending any sort of lesson. Yes, this includes ball caps.

7. If you invite your instructor to attend your show, it is proper protocol for you to purchase a ticket for him or her. In the case of a saloon or nightclub with a cocktail minimum, you must also pick up the check for their drinks. You will also increase the odds that your teacher will attend. (Did I mention I love a tasteful bottle of elderberry?)

8. Keep to a minimum the amount of baggage you haul into the dance studio.

9. In rainy or snowy weather, you must remove your overshoes or street shoes in the cloakroom, and keep them off the dance floor.

10. Cell phones and beepers must be turned off during class, especially if they ring in a Country and Western tune. Really?

11. Keep your water bottles capped and away from the dance floor, as they could be dangerous.

12. If you are a beginner, you may not participate in an advanced class, so forget about even asking. Otherwise, be prepared for a curt, "What are you—nuts?"

13. Be punctual for dance class. You mustn't miss the warm-up, lest people might think you're from The Dolly Dinkle School of Dance.

14. If it is an adult dance class, youngsters are not allowed—not even as guests.

15. Chewing gum is not allowed in any dance, singing, acting, or speech class. No gum. Please.

16. Hair must be clean and off the face and neck for every kind of lesson. Voice, dance, and acting teachers need to look for expression, and signs of tension, they must also observe the line of the body.

17. You mustn't wear jewelry to dance class.

18. Learn the dress code for class and dress as requested. Loose -fitting clothing is preferred for voice and acting classes, but won't do for dance class.

19. The proper way for ballet class to begin is with every student standing with their left hand on the barre.

20. The touching of mirrors or hanging and leaning on the ballet barre is barbaric and will get you sent to the cloakroom along with the Dolly Dinkle folks.

21. No talking whatsoever in dance class. Visiting freely is strictly taboo.

22. Raise your hand when you have a question in dance lessons.

23. Keep your tap shoes silent when the teacher is speaking. (In 1898, Dick Handy was tapping while his teacher, Miss Maudie, was trying to talk.

Maudie smacked him in the gob with a Capezio pump! Poor Dick never fully recovered and became a drummer in Dubuque.)

24. Have some circular awareness in dancing class. You aren't the only one in the room who is dancing. And if you aren't dancing, stand aside for those who are.

25. Stay in the formations and lines that have been established in your dance lessons. You mustn't take up an unreasonable amount of space.

26. It is a mortal sin not to stay for the duration of the dance class. Trips to the lavatory, cloakroom or the bubble fountain are disruptive and not abided.

27. It is traditional to applaud vigorously for the instructor at the end of the class.

Stick with my rules of etiquette for your lessons, and I, Prudence Pickle, will guarantee that you will be starting your career off on the right foot!

CHAPTER TWO
Audition Etiquette

1. Be prompt for your auditions. This means you must arrive at least ten minutes before your audition. You will need ample time to fill out the audition form. (Incidentally, the audition monitors are often the stage managers for the show you are auditioning for. You want to make the right impression.)

2. If you are going to be tardy for your audition, you must ring them up and let them know.

3. When you are in the waiting room, respect the other actors' need to concentrate and keep your chatting to a minimum.

4. This would not be a grand time to work out the kinks in your music hall act.

5. You are expected to bring a photo and resume with you to every audition, even if they know you well and have you on file.

6. If it is a musical you are auditioning for, you must have a few extra songs on hand.

7. Have all the music in the correct key in a three-ring notebook. Clearly mark where you begin and end.

8. My darlings, in your own good interests, you MUSTN'T snap your fingers at the accompanist. (In 1910, the famous tenor, Sir Edwin, "Upstage," was snapping away at the Mistro Derefinko, when his digits were pulverized by Derfinko's metronome. After that? He couldn't even hail a cab!)

9. Your resume must be an indisputably truthful account of your work and training. Put just one whopper on your resume and I guarantee that the

only singing you'll be doing is to the birds in Rock Creek, Montana.

10. Be specific when filling out audition forms, particularly the section entitled "Conflicts." However, on the part where it says: "Age," you may put your age range rather than your actual age. ("3-96" is not an age range. It's a life.)

11. Regarding when to shake hands at an audition: Shake only if they offer their hand first. Be mindful when shaking hands with piano players. Wear no jumbo-size rings, and connect gently, for their fingers are their fortune.

12. When you are doing an iconic monologue, you may announce the title and character but you mustn't announce the author's name (Shakespeare), as this would be a tad insulting to the auditor's intelligence.

13. Pay heed to audition requests. If asked to bring pop music, singing *Madame Butterfly* would be the quickest way to "NEXT."

14. The polished performer will dress well for auditions. Have respect for the craft when choosing your wardrobe. As my Aunt Katty used to say: "Tis

clothes that make the maid, you know." No clomping about in boots for *Blithe Spirit*, but no ghastly ghost makeup either. Leave something to the imagination. Commercial auditions are a different breed of cat and you may costume yourself a wee bit to suggest the character.

15. Darlings, do maintain a charming demeanor even when one of the people you are reading for is eating a ham sandwich. Take it like a pro, my dears, for you mustn't have a puss on.

16. Before you leave the audition room, you must say "thank you." You must get the names of all the people you audition for and keep them on file. When you audition for them in the future and recall their names, they will be thoroughly delighted.

17. Kissing in an audition scene can be very embarrassing. Before you start, simply ask the director how they would like you to handle the kiss. Action can be awkward if one is holding a script. For a hug, simply touch the other actor's hand or shoulder.

18. At times it's a grand idea to send thank-you notes to the folks you have auditioned for. Use your common sense to determine when it would be

appropriate and when it would seem a bit "hat in hand." Keep the notes brief, use plain stationery or cards. If you choose cards with "thank you" printed on them you must be certain to include a personal note inside. You mustn't send cutsey cards either. You don't want them thinking you're from The Dolly Dinkle School of Dance. (Come to think of it, I, Prudence Pickle, knew Dolly Dinkle. She couldn't tap her way out of a paper bag, poor dear. But that's another story.)

CHAPTER THREE
Rehearsal & Performance Etiquette

1. Any theater is a temple of art. So, please, relegate your wads of gum, water bottles and any other dreck to the rubbish bin.

2. Once a scene is blocked, the next time you work on that particular scene you're expected to be off-book. This rule is standard. However,

in opera and in some stock musical companies, you're required to be off-book before rehearsals begin. I, Prudence Pickle, feel that your knowledge of the script is a black-and-white issue. You either know your lines, or you do not. There are no grey areas.

3. You are not allowed to call, "line" once the director has stipulated that the stage manager will no longer be on- book.

4. If you must walk across the room during rehearsals, you mustn't cross in front of the director's line of vision.

5. What is a "show pony"? Oh botheration! A show pony is the actor who strolls through rehearsals, saving his or her performance for "the real audience," and never delivers until opening night. At which point the pony trots out on the stage and lets loose. Directors need to see your performance well before the audience arrives. So, let's keep the show ponies in the barn, shall we?

6. Always record blocking in pencil and be open to any changes the director may give you, until the last moment. Smile, and carry a big eraser.

7. When getting a note from the director or stage manager, simply JTTN, meaning, "Just take the note." You mustn't squander the director's precious time explaining why it was imperative for you to miss your entrance. Be a pro. (See Chapter Nine : "What Does A Pro Do?")

8. Be the kind of actor that all directors love, one who only has to be given a note once.

9. Take your work seriously, but not yourself. (This little hint is simple, but quite difficult for some to follow.)

10. If you wish to be shunned by your fellow cast mates, try giving another actor a note, such as: "You should hop on one leg when you say that line." Many a donnybrook has erupted over this famous issue, so know your boundaries. Always go to the stage manager with any concerns about other actors.

11. During technical rehearsals, please eliminate the following dialogue with designers, or crew:
    - "Say, did you know that there aren't any . . . "
    - "When do we get . . . "
    - "Is THAT how it's going to look?"

- Or the worst of all, "This is too dark!"

Imagine how you would feel on your first day of rehearsal, if somebody ankled up to you and said: "Is THAT how you're going to play that part?" Goodness me.

12. It's just the dickens for lighting designers when actors wear white to technical rehearsals. White will reflect the light. You mustn't wear white.

13. Once the show has opened, you must be consistent with your performance, and true to what the director has given you to do. Surely things evolve during an extended run to keep the moments alive. However, to change the blocking or the concepts would be taboo, and very Dolly Dinkle.

14. Keep all practical jokes off the stage. Play a prank on stage and you may as well be stamping the words 'rank amatuer' on your forehead. The only laughing you'll be doing will be in East Overshoe, Wisconsin.

15. You must devote yourself to becoming a positive light around your cast and crew. Work hard at not being a nay-sayer.

16. Theatre folks are a tad superstitious about a few things. Uttering "Macbeth" out loud inside any theater is FORBIDDEN!

You may write it, but you may not speak the word out loud. It's okay to say it outside, but when inside, please refer to it as "The Scottish Play," or else you may cause a series of tragic mishaps to befall your company. This is referred to as "The Scottish Curse." If you slip and voice the dreaded word, you are required to run outside, turn around three times and spit over your left shoulder. You must also knock on the door and someone must invite you back inside. In 1856, Chauncey Tomkins got his ticket punched after receiving a blow to the head with a prompt book. The deadly book was tossed by a nearby stage manager upon hearing the word "Macbeth." (Incidentally, I worked with Chauncey when I was alive, and the man also NEVER knew his lines, chewed gum . . . and the scenery . . . lied on his resume, and probably attended The Dolly Dinkle School of Dance.)

17. Another superstition is whistling backstage, it's bad luck. You may not whistle backstage, ever. In the olden days of theatre, ages before headsets, producers would hire sailors as 'fly men.' The seamen were accustomed to working with ropes, and therefore were perfect for the duties of flying scenery. (Handsome devils they were too!) To call cues without disrupting the show, fly men would whistle to signal when a drop—canvas scenery attached to an enormous lead pipe—rolled down. Whistling backstage in those olden days was dangerous. The superstition has stuck, so whistling back stage is not done. In 1908, the famous soubrette Miss Peony Piacenti whistled back stage. Piacenti was clocked by a falling drop, and she had annoying "pauses" in her performances ever since, thus her handle, "Pauser Piacenti."

18. Oddly enough, in our business, saying: "good luck" is in fact, bad luck. artists prefer "Break a leg." In

opera they prefer "In bocca lupo." (In the mouth of the wolf.)

Dolly Dinkle prefers *Merde—French* for you-know-what. The term "Break a leg" comes from bowing. When you bow you put one foot behind the other and bend the knee. The more the audience applauds the more you bend that back leg, or "break" the line of it. Hence, if you "break a leg," you are taking a deep bow.

19. Quiet is demanded backstage for the benefit of those who are onstage.

20. If you are offstage, stay out of the sight lines of those who are on the stage.

21. On opening night it is traditional to give a small gift to your co-workers. Nobody wishes you to go to debtor's prison, so remember that a card or note would be just as lovely.

22. There is usually an opening night party and the polished pro knows that you dress appropriately, meaning eveningwear. Get gussied up and have a lovely time.

23. Respect the costumes, props and scenery. They are works of art carefully crafted by fellow theater artists.

24. When traveling behind a scrim, go slowly so it won't go higgle-dee-piggle-dee and disrupt the show.

25. Oh, the dreadful and most loathsome COPY CAT. Create your own work out there and remember: "A thoroughbred never looks at the other horses." Of course, this doesn't apply to acting with someone.

26. Be a generous actor and share the stage.

27. All conflicts boil down to the same thing every time. You are either a professional or you are not. The next time you are involved in a conflict, stop and ask yourself: "Am I a professional in this situation, or not?"

28. During technical rehearsals, keep your belongings off the floor and out of the aisles. directors and staff are constantly moving about checking the sight-lines.

29. Question-and-answer sessions with the audiences aren't your own personal interviews. You mustn't hog the show.

30. Accept compliments gracefully, especially from the audience—even if you had a beastly evening.

*I, **Prudence Pickle**, simply adore actors who respect their audience. **Keep my rules in mind and you will be keeping your career in a good light, and we thespians love our light, don't we?***

CHAPTER FOUR

Dressingroom Etiquette

1. When the stage manager gives you your calls, you must respond so they may know you heard their call. If you really care to impress your stage manager (and you do), the following is the proper way to respond: SM: "Five minutes, Miss Pickle." Miss P: "Thank you, five."

2. When working at the dressing table or costume rack, be aware of where you work- space begins and ends.

3. Playing music in the dressing room after "half hour" is unseemly, and not allowed. Ear buds are frowned upon as well.

4. Using hair spray or any other aerosol in the dressing room is out. It constricts the throat. You must dash outside the room and spray. Opera singers are famous for getting into donnybrooks over this issue. Why, once in 1885 when the incomparable Mezzo "Wheezer" Lipschitz was being sewn into her corset, she was suddenly overtaken by a soprano's perfume. Sadly, the soprano Miss Amendolia, was later discovered hanging from the pin rail by her own fishnets.

5. It is not *de rigueur* to discuss reviews—grand or devastating—in the dressing room.

6. Maintain a countenance of good humor in the dressingroom and avoid engaging in gossip.

7. Dressers are not your servants. Please hang up your costumes and treat these people like gold.

8. Learn how to handle your ventilated wig so that you won't (gasp!) rip the netting. Wig masters are frequently committed to sanitariums to recover from having to hand-tie your lovely wig. Hair by teeny-tiny hair.

9. Well-bred actors know to ask the other people in the cast if they wish to know when notable people are in the audience and respond accordingly.

10. Whenever a well-known actor, director, producer, or agent visits you backstage, it is gracious to introduce this person to any cast members who happen to be around.

11. You may not have friends or relatives in the dressing room before or after the show.

12. It is best to keep your cell phone off after "half hour."

13. It is expected of you to give a gratuity to your dresser and wig person. A charming gift at the end of the run is also fine. Many people join together on a group tip based on how many shows are worked. The technical rehearsals must also be included.

14. The stage door person is usually tipped when you are on the road, as they are calling cabs for you,

providing local information, security, delivering your flowers, and other niceties.

15. You simply mustn't borrow another actor's makeup. Particularly eye makeup. This is a great way to spread around monstrous infections.

16. If you must borrow a pencil sharpener, clean it after using it.

17. Keep your conversation light in the dressing room. Be a pro, even if your life is a veritable shipwreck. (See Chapter Nine, "What Does A Pro Do?")

18. Avoid discussing auditions in the dressing room. Keep these tidbits to yourself and that way you won't be finding forks in your tights.

19. Oh, dear! You simply mustn't be late for "half hour," but if it's unavoidable, ring up the stage manager beforehand and let him know.

Follow my rules for the dressing room, and I, Prudence Pickle, will be honored to share a space with you.

CHAPTER FIVE

Understudy Etiquette

1. Be an excellent understudy and stay in the background.

2. You mustn't discuss the health and well-being of the person you are covering.

3. You mustn't ever be in the sight lines of the person you are covering while shadowing them during the show.

4. If you replace someone, your first responsibility is to make this transition as seamless as possible for the other company members.

5. It is imperative that you be cordial and classy. You must say something complimentary about both the actor you are replacing and the show you are going into. It would be a sign of ill breeding if you didn't compliment the other actors in the show you are stepping into. (Hubert Egbert Morrissey neglected this nicety, and other than selling roses out of the back of his secondhand Volkswagen, Hubert hasn't done much lately.)

6. Anytime you go backstage after a performance and the actors have just come off stage dripping with perspiration (no need to point this out), say something positive to all you see or else get thee gone. I, Prudence Pickle, worked with Hubert Egbert Morrissey in stock and I can assure you that he found many a fork in his tights.

CHAPTER SIX

Etiquette on a Movie Set

1. If you wish to watch a scene being filmed that you aren't in, you must first ask the second assistant director.

2. When observing the filming of another scene, you mustn't ever be in the actors' sight lines.

3. A movie set is very much like a kingdom. People are very territorial concerning chairs in this kingdom. Check the back of the chair and if you don't find your name there, you mustn't sit in it. If you aren't a regular, your chair will most likely be the one that says: "Guest." Always ask the second assistant director which guest chair is yours.

4. You are not allowed to leave your pocketbook or other belongings on the set.

5. Sound instruments are highly capable, so when the bell rings or they say "sound" (They used to say "roll em."), be silent. You begin the scene when they call "action." The quickest way to feel like a nickel would be to ignore this rule.

6. Any kind of movement can be a distraction when shooting, so no waltzing about while another scene is being filmed.

7. When an actor is finished filming and it's announced that they have "wrapped," the crew has

a charming tradition of applauding for them. You must clap for them as well.

8. It's not a good plan to bring friends and family along with you to the set.

9. If you are a minor, you must always have one parent or guardian with you on set at all times.

10. Check with the second assistant director before dragging camcorders, cameras or any recording device on the set.

11. If you are hired as an extra, you are not allowed to speak to the actors who have roles. Remember now, it is a kingdom and extras are considered the lowest on the food-chain. So, if you wish to be an extra, grow a thick skin, and take it on the chin.

12. If you are an extra, know your place. (No, if you are playing a dead person, you mustn't rise from the dead. Hee-hee!)

13. Always be on time or five or ten minutes early.

14. You must come to the set knowing your lines.

15. You must hang up your costumes.

I, Prudence Pickle, hope you will keep these rules in your pocket book and avoid any unpleasant words from the traditionally discourteous second assistant directors.

CHAPTER SEVEN

Interpersonal Theater Etiquette

1. If you wish to use a coach or teacher as a credit on
    your resume, you must first ask their permission.

2. If you ask someone to write a letter of recommendation for you, it is proper to send him or her a little gift in return. A gift card to a bookstore is a pleasing way to express your gratitude. If you have no financial resources, then a professional, classy, card will do the job. ringing him up, emailing, texting, twittering (whatever that is) is very "Dolly Dinkle," and will simply not suffice.

3. When a well-known performer is in your audience, it is customary, if possible, to have him announced to the audience prior to the show. When working in night clubs, you must always have this sort of announcement made.

4. It is important to find out exactly how the person of note prefers to be introduced. It would be most gracious of you to also include a short plug for whatever show they are currently doing. Well-known performers have earned this recognition. I, Prudence Pickle, must insist that you show respect to seasoned performers.

CHAPTER EIGHT
Child Actors and their Parents

1. You must pay heed to any audition instructions put out by the theater, particularly the section where it says: "NO CALLS." Dear Readers, I took special care to place this pearl first, because it is the worst mistake you can possibly make. No matter how gifted your little Ermengarde may be, badgering the casting office will send up a red flag and could cost her the job.

2. It is customary to always send a note or a small token of your appreciation to all people who recommended your dear Zaneeta for the job.

3. If your Cornelius is cast, he must understand that he is representing the people who recommended him and must therefore exhibit exemplary behavior.

4. Inform everyone who aided your Elphaba in getting the job (i.e. casting people, agents, teachers, etc.) that she has landed the part and thank him or her with a handwritten note, of course.

5. Always be a model of first-class behavior for your child whenever discussing the other children under consideration for a role. Teach Dilbert early on to honor his fellow artists.

6. Sneaking in to spy on rehearsals is exceedingly destructive. With a parent peering around, kids will want to perform before they are ready or worse, they will clam up. You must give dear Barnaby a break and bring along a book.

7. You mustn't play director—that is if you wish sweet Winifred to be rehired.

8. Do drop your darling Dewdrop off on time. And pick her up on time, too! Anything less is an inconvenience. Teachers aren't nannies, and child wranglers aren't paid overtime. Promptness is greatly appreciated.

9. Before committing your young artist to a contract or recital, peruse the schedule first. Announcing mid-rehearsal that Eulalie has to dash off to London for a wedding is highly problematic. Be a doll, respect the job.

10. Regarding class work: It is highly unprofessional to interfere with any skill level placements the teacher may make. (Assuming you aren't sending poor, unfortunate Dirwood to the dreaded Dolly Dinkle School of Dance).

11. If precious Paris or Peoria gets cast in a movie or television show, do read my chapter on movie set etiquette post haste.

12. Make sure your young actor doesn't hear any negative feedback about his or her audition. However, constructive criticism delivered carefully and preceded by positive comments is fine. Explain to your Galinda, in a child's terms, that she must not take it

personally when she does not get the job. Suggest that she may be too tall or too short, etc. You could also explain that she needs to increase her options and go to more auditions. Continuing training and working on her craft will also increase her odds.

13. Sometimes sharing positive feedback with Adelaide can have a devastating effect on her. How? If she hears "They loved you," she may come to believe that when she doesn't get that same feedback that therefore "They hated her."

14. Please make it crystal-clear to your child that you love them whether they get the part or not.

In conclusion, Moms and Dads, I, Prudence Pickle, want to remind you of the importance of showing extra affection to your other children who don't act. With all the fuss over Kumquat every time she has an audition, your other youngsters will be in need of some special attention. And if Kumquat is cast in a movie it may be possible for the other kids to be extras, so do ask. (The second assistant director will be kinder to children.)

CHAPTER NINE
What Does a Pro Do?

1. A pro shows respect for writers and does not paraphrase.

2. A pro shows respect for composers and learns the music exactly as written.

3. A pro is always on time and usually early.

4. A pro always knows his lines blocking, etc., when required to.

5. A pro is vigilant about taking care of his instrument by staying healthy, fit and flexible.

6. A pro gets off of his rusty dusty and goes to class.

7. A pro, when ill, will be mindful not to spread his disease to others.

8. A pro keeps an open mind, an open heart, and is adaptable.

9. A pro will always give a kind word to the actors when he goes backstage after a show.

10. A pro is exciting to watch and wouldn't dream of "phoning in" his performance.

11. A pro isn't overly competitive. He is wise enough to know that you must surround yourself with the best and learn from them all.

12. A pro maintains the integrity of the show that the director has guided him to.

13. A pro is always warmed up for the show.

14. A pro doesn't bring his problems to the theater.

15. A pro is quiet backstage.

16. A pro will treat his props, costumes, scenery, and any other work of art or equipment with respect.

17. A pro always checks his props before the show.

18. A pro knows that the stage manager's word is likened to the Word of the Lord.

19. A pro always respects his audience.

20. A pro knows the proper behavior to exhibit backstage, and in the dressingroom.

21. A pro doesn't engage in gossiping.

22. A pro will not tend be a negative sort of chap.

23. A pro understands the value of going to watch other performers.

24. A pro is a pleasure to know, a pleasure to work with and a pleasure to watch.

25. A pro has class and the polished deportment that he acquired from reading my book. *Etiquette for Professional Actors.*

Before You Go . . .

My rules of etiquette arise from a high regard and fondness for actors and their craft, which is the backbone of my charming Pickle Method. As with all good etiquette, these rules are about professionalism, goodness, civility, and love—and not about being an elitist.

Tendering these courtesies will help you to avoid a painful semester or two in the School of Hard Knocks.

Follow the Pickle method to a graceful life in the theater and do pack this book in your grip whenever you go out on a tour. I, Prudence Pickle, wish you a long and lovely career.

Break a leg.
Fondly,

Prudence Pickle
Prudence Pickle

Ghost Light:

A ghost light is a tall metal stand with a large light bulb hanging inside a cage. This lamp is turned on at night after the show is over—or, in theater talk, "dark." The light is left center stage close to the edge by the orchestra pit, better known as "down center." The purpose of the ghost light is to prevent people from stumbling in the dark, or falling into the orchestra pit.

This device also has a lot of superstition attached to it. In the olden days, actors were thought to be a sinful lot, and therefore their souls were doomed to remain on earth haunting old theaters. To this day, the ghost light is left on at night when the theaters are dark, so the spirits of actors can come out and play or rather "tread the boards."

This book is dedicated to Thomas Q. Morris and the memory of Lorraine Bronson, and Audrey Stottler.

Special thanks goes to Thomas Q. Morris. Without Tom's guidance, generosity, and brilliant contributions, this book would never have been written. Thanks also to Michelle Berg who encouraged, prodded, and became the engine behind this project. Thank you to my talented sister Paddy O'Connell MacDonald for her support and line editing. Thank you to Michelle and Raymond Berg for their editing. Thanks also to Stephanie Zimbalist, Nancy Tabor, my parents, Donna and Geoff O'Connell, Timmy and Naomi O'Connell, Rhonda Smith, Mary Howarth, Kerry Casserly—and Dolly Dinkle for her unique contributions.

Made in the USA
Columbia, SC
31 December 2019

85852329R00030